Pra

"A book of g... every word ...beauty of the numan spirit. I was moved and inspired by this heartfelt and honest account of the daily challenges facing Christine on her journey. I heartily recommend this book, rich with memorable life lessons to anyone wishing to deal with many of life's most difficult experiences in a deeply meaningful way."

Susan Elsey, BA, RSW
CNIB

"Christine has taken her experiences and allowed all of us a chance to see what life can be like when you are faced with serious challenges. This book is a testament to Christine's incredible ability to show courage and determination in the face of adversity. Christine has a strong commitment to her family and her community - we all do good things in life, but some of us strive to do great things, and Christine is one of these people. Thank you, Christine for inviting us into your world."

Curtis Wyatt, President Wyatt Dowling
Insurance Brokers and Friend.

Christine M. Bonnett

The Patient PATIENT

To Brett

Cheers! Christina

THE PATIENT PATIENT
Copyright © 2013 by Christine M. Bonnett

All rights reserved. Neither this publication nor any part of this publication may be reproduced or transmitted in any form or by any means, electronic or mechanical, including photocopying, recording or any information storage and retrieval system, without permission in writing from the author.

Cover art: Rhian Brynjolson

ISBN: 978-1-4866-0214-8

Word Alive Press
131 Cordite Road, Winnipeg, MB R3W 1S1
www.wordalivepress.ca

Cataloguing in Publication may be obtained through Library and Archives Canada

Dedication

To my husband Barry, who chose to love me and stay by my side. I'm still trying to figure out what I did to deserve such a caring life partner. You stuck with me through all the medical roadblocks, the outdated waiting room magazines, and the unknown that confronted our marriage daily. I owe you my undying love and respect.

To my brother Dan (1956–2002), who was my mentor and showed me that life does go on after diagnosis. Dan wouldn't allow his illness to prevent him from living his life to the fullest and he became a role model for many living with a chronic illness. For being my greatest role model, I will be forever thankful.

Contents

Foreword	xi
Prologue	xv
Introduction	xvii

1.	The Neighbourhood	1
2.	Shh! Don't Tell Mom And Dad!	7
3.	Diagnosis—Lupus, The Disease Of A Thousand Faces	11
4.	Dad	23
5.	Diagnosis—Optic Neuritis	31
6.	Hospital Stays	37
7.	The Break-In	45
8.	Dan	49
9.	The Middle East	55
10.	Back To Work	59
11.	British Isles	63
12.	And Then There Were Four	67
13.	Going Blind	73
14.	Romance In The Yukon	83
15.	Radio Show	87
16.	Lost?	91
17.	Diagnosis—Neuromyelitis Optica (NMO)	95

18. H1N1—Isolation   115

Epilogue   121

Author's Note

Throughout the book, you will notice song titles at the beginning of every chapter. Some of my earliest memories are of music and the events that surrounded me hearing it. I don't just mean at weddings, funerals, or birthday parties. I mean the kind of music you hear in everyday—like my brothers playing Led Zeppelin upstairs or my mom and dad playing their Scottish music downstairs. Music is very emotional for me. In fact, almost everybody in my life can be represented with a song or type of music.

Foreword

As a neurologist, I have had the distinct pleasure of meeting many different people with varied personalities and life experiences. I also have the opportunity to observe how they deal with the daily challenges borne of living with chronic illness.

    I first met Christine Bonnett about five years ago, at the time when she was newly diagnosed with neuromyelitis optica, an event that happened relatively late in her story. Although neuromyelitis optica may be misdiagnosed as a severe form of multiple sclerosis, it is a different disease, and it is much less common. The rarity of the condition can often lead affected individuals to feel isolated and unsupported.

Neuromyelitis optica characteristically attacks the nerves to the eyes, leading to visual impairment, and in some cases, like Christine's, to complete blindness. This disease also affects the spinal cord, and consequently may lead to numbness and weakness in the limbs, pain, spasms, and difficulty walking, among other symptoms.

Unfortunately, these are not the only challenges Christine has had to face; however, she has dealt with all of these challenges with a characteristically sarcastic wit, and a fierce desire to retain control over her life and to use her experiences to help others.

This story is important for all of us, with its universal themes of suffering and loss, and because it illustrates the impact that a supportive social circle and attitude make. In the words of John Donne,

> *"No man is an island,*
> *Entire of itself,*
> *Every man is a piece of the continent,*

Foreword

> *A part of the main.*
> *If a clod be washed away by the sea,*
> *Europe is the less.*
> *As well as if a promontory were.*
> *As well as if a manor of thy friend's*
> *Or of thine own were:*
> *Any man's [struggle] diminishes me,*
> *Because I am involved in mankind,*
> *And therefore never send to know*
> *for whom the bell tolls;*
> *It tolls for thee."*
> —John Donne, *Meditation XVII*
> English clergyman and poet (1572–1631)

Although some specific illnesses are mentioned in this book, it is not really a book about those illnesses, nor is it a book about miraculous recoveries or saccharine happy endings. This book presents the realities of Christine's journey with family and friends, and her perspectives about that journey. Mostly, though, it is a book about resilience, coping, and hope.

Hope is the thing with feathers, that perches in the soul, and sings the tune without the words, and never stops at all.[1]

Enjoy.
—Ruth Ann Marrie, MD, PhD
Associate Professor of Medicine
University of Manitoba
Winnipeg, Manitoba
2013

---

[1] Emily Dickinson, Complete Poems (1924). Part One: Life XXXII.

Prologue

I played a number of sports growing up—volleyball, basketball, ping pong, and so on. However, the most memorable was baseball. What made baseball so memorable wasn't so much the game, but the girls I played with (and our tomato-red uniforms). When we were all together having the time of our lives, we believed nothing could stop us. The world was our oyster and we took things for granted—especially our health.

    I recently attended my high school reunion, and many of these girls were there. We spoke of baseball memories more than school. We talked about how we had to have our hair and makeup "just right" in case any boys showed up to watch us play.

We talked about the different coaches we had over the years, my brother Dan being one of them for two seasons. We couldn't all agree on specific details of these stories, but the one thing we could agree on was the fights. When you think about girls' baseball, you don't think about fighting, but there were some humzingers!

Little did I know about the personal fight I would soon be facing.

Not too long after high school, I began the long, often scary journey of learning to never take things for granted. No one knows what the future holds; all we have is today.

This is my story.

Introduction

"We Are Family" (Sister Sledge)

Had you told me ten years ago that I'd be writing a book, I might have laughed at you, looked at you with a stunned expression on my face, or simply said you were crazy. But here we are. So who's the crazy one?

I never thought I had anything in my life worth writing about. I'm doing this for a couple of reasons. The first is purely therapeutic. The second is to hopefully reach out to even one person who may benefit from reading my story.

I grew up in a small wartime house in Winnipeg, Manitoba—more specifically, the most eastern area, called Transcona. I had a relatively normal childhood. Allow me to

Dad with Belle and Babe

introduce the Slessor family, descendants of Scottish immigrants.

My father, George, lived most of his life in Transcona and worked as a delivery driver for a local lumber company. In his younger years, he owned a team of Clydesdales (Belle and Babe) and would hook them up to a sleigh in the winter. He would do "Tally Ho's" for the church youth groups. I can totally see my dad doing this, as he was a patient man who loved young people and children.

My mom, Margaret, grew up on a farm in Elie, Manitoba. In fact, Mom and Dad met at a wedding social in Elie.[2] Mom, for the most part, was a housewife and occasionally took on odd jobs to help with the bills. Usually these jobs would involve cleaning the neighbourhood doctor's office or motel.

Money was scarce, but food was always plenty. We never went hungry. Mom was unbelievable with money—she could really stretch a dollar!

My Family Values

Love is such a big word, feeling, or value. As the youngest of five children—and also the only girl—I had a unique outlook. Before you ask, the answer is yes, I was spoiled. Every Christmas, there were loads of presents under the tree. I was oblivious to the church hampers being delivered to the door, as my father was laid off for a few months nearly every winter. I had no idea

---

[2] For those of you who didn't grow up in Manitoba, a wedding social is a fundraising dance to help the couple-to-be pay for the wedding.

of our gloomy financial situation. My parents and brothers made sure of that. As an adult, now knowing the truth, I am in awe of my family. The love they had for me and for each other to make sure a little girl enjoyed her Christmas without skipping a beat makes me beam with pride.

My parents were very huggy and affectionate with each other, and probably not the way other people were. Dad would chase Mom around the house to put ice down the back of her shirt. She would pretend to be angry about it, but he always made her laugh. He could always get me. When I was so angry at him I could spit, all he would have to do was poke me in the arm and say, "Smile if you love me." I would get even angrier that he was almost mocking me. As a teenager, I thought he was so weird. He never did play fair. I think he reserved these displays of affection for Mom and me, as the only females in the family. It's regrettable that he was of the era when you didn't show a lot of affection to boys. I'm sure he did when they were very young, through roughhousing. I think my brothers knew he loved them and was proud of them.

Honesty is a value we all hold dear. We would never think of cheating someone, or lying to get what we want. Good or bad, what you see is what you get. When my brothers were young, one of them broke the furnace, but no one owned up to it. My dad lined all four of them up and asked one last time who had done it: silence. He then said, "Then all you of you will have to be punished." I can only imagine the looks on the faces of the boys who really hadn't committed the crime. So Dad slowly started taking off his belt, hoping that the guilty boy would come forward for fear of his brothers getting punished. All four boys ended up getting punished, and to this day my brothers still argue about the facts in this story—but we know my brother Scot was the guilty party.

Our parents never tried to shield us from life. Even at a young age, they would be honest about a death in the family and try their best to help us understand. They would rarely sugar coat things. Basically, we had to learn to cope. Death is a part of life; that was their philosophy. This ideal aided me tremendously when my health started to fail. I tried, and am still trying, to remain positive. I know it's a cliché, but staying real is the best way to help me articulate my thoughts when I'm working through difficult circumstances in my life.

Respect was an important priority in our house. To this day, I can still hear my dad telling me to always respect my elders. The respect that was instilled in us as kids naturally flowed over into all our relationships. This respect was evident even in our relationship with our pets. My parents grew up on a farm and were around animals all their lives. My father demanded respect from them, but expected us to respect that they were different and had feelings also. From this, we all have a great love and respect for animals and nature.

My Dad also felt it was *very* important to respect our mother. He understood we would have conflicts with both of our parents, but

Introduction

Mom and Dad dating – February, 1954

if that respect line was ever crossed when speaking with Mom, he intervened and let us know that we were treading on thin ice. My brothers have always respected women and the relationship they have with their wives. It's neat to see a little of Dad in them when their kids disrespect their mom in some way.

My mother had a different bent on respect. Her hope was that we would always want to respect family traditions, anything from family dinners, visiting grandparents and older relatives, and giving Christmas cards to remembering someone's birthday. The first Christmas without Mom was very difficult. I really missed the traditions she brought to our family. I especially missed baking with her during the two weeks before Christmas—just the two of us in her small kitchen baking butter tarts, fudge, and decorating gingerbreads with Gene Autry Christmas music playing in the background.

A **strong work ethic** is something I hope I have embraced through my family. My parents both performed manual labour all their lives. We were taught to give it our all, no matter the job or project. Pride relates to this also. Being from the old school, my father would have really liked to see my brothers get into a trade. This would usually mean something that involved working with their hands. He really respected a man who could put in a hard day's work.

When my husband Barry and I were engaged, Dad called him one day to go with him on a delivery. Dad would usually deliver outside of Winnipeg; he knew every small town in Manitoba. Barry agreed to join him, as he wanted to develop a relationship with my dad. Being alone in a truck for a few hours was a great way to do that. When they arrived at their first stop, Barry jumped out to start helping Dad unload sheets of drywall. Did I mention that Barry is 6'3" and was twenty years old at the time? Dad was in his early sixties and 5'2". Before Barry knew it, Dad had picked up the first large sheet by himself and threw it over his shoulder. Barry, trying to impress his future father-in-law, knew he would have to at least keep up. He did, but he sure paid for it the following day with a sore back. That was the day Dad knew Barry was a keeper.

Dad took all of us kids on deliveries through the years. It was almost a privilege to be asked. After years of hearing all the stories of the road, I could hardly wait for my turn to take part in this: the Slessor family rite of passage. Even though Dad was from the old school, he knew that a woman needed to be independent and take care of herself.

Mom was also an incredibly hard worker. At one point, she was maintaining the house for the seven of us, working two evenings a week, and then both she and Dad worked as weekend custodians at the local community club. Looking back, I was never embarrassed of the types of jobs they took to take care of us. It never even entered my mind.

It didn't matter to our parents what we did for work. We all had varied jobs through the years—deejay, radio announcer, electrician, donut shop clerk, waitress, case worker, orderly, construction crew, among others. The fact that we were supporting ourselves was pride enough for our parents. My dad wasn't the type to tell you to your face that he was proud of you, but we found it interesting that his buddies all knew what we were up to. From that, we knew he was proud. Mom was the type to say she was proud of me and tell me that she had always been proud of me and all my brothers. I can already see my brothers, who are now fathers, instilling this ethic in their own children.

Gracious. I had to ask a couple of old family friends for this one. I asked them what they think of when they consider our family. The word "gracious" came up. We all have a knack for organizing all sorts of gatherings. We are all people people. We love to socialize and participate in events. We aren't exactly shy! We also love to entertain in our homes.

One Thanksgiving about twenty-five years ago, my brother Dan called Mom to ask if she minded him bringing a friend home for dinner, since this friend was in Winnipeg to attend university and had no family here. Without even a second thought, Mom said, "You better bring her!"

Dan was in line at the bookstore and met Sabrina there. If anyone has ever been in a bookstore line at university, you know you may be there for a while. He started talking to this girl and found out that she was new to the city and didn't know many people. He actually invited her right then and there, as he knew Mom would welcome her with open arms. I'm sure we overwhelmed her, but I think she was glad she came; my other brother Jack thought she was cute and wanted to call her for a date afterwards. Well, they have been together ever since and have two beautiful daughters.

    That's us in a nutshell.

1.

THE NEIGHBOURHOOD

"These Are The People In My Neighbourhood"
(Sesame Street)

The neighbourhood I grew up in was unique. I think we had fifty kids in a one-block radius. At the end of our street was a city park. On Saturdays, every mother on the block knew to find their kids there. The older kids would play baseball while checking in on their younger siblings in the red and white canopy-covered sandbox. We would be at the park as early as 9:00 a.m. but only stay as late as 5:00 p.m., because that's when we all ran home to watch Bugs Bunny.

Most families in my neighbourhood were large and in the lower middle income bracket. Needless to say, few of us could afford air-conditioning in the summer. During the really hot days, it was cooler outside than inside and you would catch more than a handful of neighbours sitting on their steps trying to keep cool. As kids, we also had the most awesome hide-and-seek games. I felt bad for the seeker because of the sheer numbers he or she would have to find.

The neighbourhood was home to many of my first experiences. I had my first driving lesson in a 1967 Pontiac (the boat) with my dad. My first lesson in perogy-making with Mrs. D was a prerequisite. I'm sure I failed the lesson but passed enjoying and eating them. There was my first bacon mushroom pizza from Dal's Restaurant, which I still enjoy today. I had my first street hockey game—and my first kiss. My first kiss was the most romantic moment of my sixteen-year-old life and happened while I was sitting on a swing in the park at the end of the street. A girl never forgets. Thanks, Tony!

Although Mom baked throughout the year, the best times I remember are the cold winter days, getting up in the morning and smelling the dough my mom was preparing for fresh buns, and seeing the crock pot she would make homemade soup in. This gave my day a boost, knowing what I would be in for when I got home from school. She would use the last bit of dough to make cinnamon buns that could be smelled all the way down the back lane.

Halloween in my neighbourhood was incredible. Halloween night had almost the same excitement and anticipation as Christmas Eve. Living in a cold climate like the one in Winnipeg, we usually had snow on the ground before Halloween, so our costumes had to fit over our winter clothes. I remember me and my friends trick-or-treating using old pillowcases to carry our treasure trove of treats. People in the neighbourhood had already started to put up Christmas lights, which made everything bright, colourful, and magical.

On Christmas morning, phone calls would begin between me and my friends. We would compare our gifts, and if a gift was really cool we would all converge at that person's house to check it out. Usually

The Patient Patient

Me (age 10) and Scot at Christmas

Kim was the first to come over, as she lived right next door and could just slip on her coat and boots over her pyjamas.

In a lot of ways, my neighbourhood was like any other neighbourhood. We had a grumpy old man who would stare at you and creep you out. You knew not to go on his lawn or in his yard; if you did, there'd be hell to pay.

There was always something going on—a bunch of us skipping, playing hopscotch, or maybe tetherball (if we could find a tree to tie the tetherball on). When I talk to other people about the neighbourhoods they grew up in, they usually turn out to have never known their neighbours—either that or they think my neighbourhood was one of a kind. I chuckle a little bit when I hear that. Maybe I was lucky. It was different. It was fun.

This must sound like I grew up in *Leave it to Beaver* or *The Cosby Show*. The truth is, I'm not in denial. We had our share of fights, just like with any big extended family. We didn't always get along. There were incidents throughout the years, including a couple of doozies, but I chose not to write about those; they don't stick in my mind.

2.

SHH! DON'T TELL MOM AND DAD!

"Does Your Mother Know?" (ABBA)

There are many incidents in my life that involve mishaps, and sometimes blood—but surprisingly, I have never had a broken bone.

My earliest recollection was when I was four or five and my brothers Jack and Scot were babysitting me. I was watching TV and they were in the kitchen doing dishes. A glass broke and they cleaned it up. Mom and Dad then phoned and I ran to the phone, wanting to talk to them. While I was talking, I looked down and saw blood trickling from my toes, obviously from splinters of glass that hadn't yet been cleaned up. Just before I screamed, one brother put his hand over my mouth and took me into the living room. My other brother grabbed the phone to tell our parents that I had gone off to see what was on TV. When my brother came to the living room to tend to my feet, I heard, for the first time, "Shh! Don't tell Mom and Dad!"

The next time I heard that was when I went to the park with Jack and his friend Larry. I was only five years old. They put me on a swing and Jack gave me an under-duck push. There I was, swinging, and at this point I was just gliding and hugging the chains loosely. Larry didn't realize that I didn't have a firm grip on the chains when he came up behind and gave me another under-duck. Suddenly, I tumbled head over heels. As blood poured out of my head, Jack's first words were, "My dad's going to kill me!" Then, "Shh! Don't tell Mom and Dad!"

Another time, another brother. I was with Norm and Sharon. I got in the car and was sitting on Sharon's lap when she closed the door on my hand. I didn't react immediately, at least not until I looked at it and realized, "Boy, that should hurt!" Then I started to cry. They opened the door and Norm pulled me over. I sat between them. They said, "Shh! Don't tell Mom and Dad!" I don't recall where we were going that day or why I was even in the car with them, but I remember Norm playing April Wine and singing it to me. So it is not a terrible memory.

When I was a bit older (about eight), I hung out with a girl down the street. They had a corner store and the family who lived there had a daughter my age. We became friends. I went out with their family one day and we were heading south on Main Street, turning west onto Portage Avenue, when the door flew open and I rolled out of the car at the corner of Portage and Main! I knew enough to get to the side of the road, but I started to cry. I didn't know where I was. I had no money to call anybody and they were nowhere in sight. In actuality, they had gone around the block to come and get me. My friend was crying because she thought I had gone under the car; these were the days when nobody wore seatbelts. I sure wore my seatbelt all the way home. I spent the night at their place. They gave me a jar of pennies and said, "There's no need to tell your parents about this." That was their version of "Shh! Don't tell Mom and Dad!"

In high school during drama class, I once leaned against a light pole but the light wasn't secured to the pole. This light fell on my head. The wound started to bleed like crazy all over me, pouring onto the new blouse I had bought! I didn't care that I'd gotten hurt, but my blouse was ruined. The vice-principal took me to my doctor's office, where I got a few stitches and had to get some of my hair shaved. I was sixteen, so this was not a good time to get my hair shaved. Again, my vice-principal was adamant about me not bothering my mom at work, as he would make sure I was taken care of. In other words, once again, "Shh! Don't tell Mom and Dad!"

3.

DIAGNOSIS—LUPUS, THE DISEASE OF A THOUSAND FACES

"Glory Of Love" (Peter Cetera)

On April 17, 1991, at the age of twenty-three, I first heard of systemic lupus erythematosus, known to the general public as lupus.[3] You never forget the

---

[3] "Lupus—also known as systemic lupus erythematosus—is a disease of the immune system. Normally, the immune system protects the body from infection. In lupus, however, the immune system inappropriately attacks tissues in various parts of the body. This abnormal activity leads to tissue damage and illness" (from "Lupus Overview," *WebMD*, September 16, 2013 [http://lupus.webmd.com/arthritis-lupus]). "The pathophysiologic characteristics of [lupus] includes severe vasculitis, renal involvement, and lesions of the skin and nervous system" (from "Systemic lupus erythematosus [SLE]," *The Free Dictionary*, September 25, 2013 [http://medical-dictionary.thefreedictionary.com/systemic+lupus+erythematosus]. Vasculitis: "an inflammatory condition of the blood vessels that is characteristic

date you are told you are living with a chronic illness. This diagnosis came about when I complained of the following symptoms: joint pain, a red rash across the bridge of my nose, weight gain, fatigue, and a reaction to sunlight. I went home and told my then-fiancé Barry. Lupus? What was that? Never heard of it. We both were rather laid back about it. Ignorance allowed us to be calm at the time.

The following day, Barry visited his mother, who was a nurse. He told her our news and immediately she began to fill him in on the details of this disease. They both ended up having a good cry, thinking I only had ten good years left. The information she had was from her outdated nursing textbooks. When Barry came home, he proceeded to give me the lowdown on this disease I now had to live with. He was almost upset with me for taking it all so lightly. Honestly, I'd had no idea.

---

of certain systemic diseases or is caused by an allergic reaction" (from "Vasculitis," *The Free Dictionary*, September 26, 2013 [http://medical-dictionary.thefreedictionary.com/vasculitis]).

The disease began to hit home when it started interfering in our social events.

Barry and I belonged to a bowling league that met every second Saturday. It was a fun time with friends that generally ended with us going out for food and drinks. On one of these bowling nights, shortly after being diagnosed with lupus, I was having a flare-up where the rash across my nose appeared. I felt sluggish and the joints in my hands were hurting so badly I was having a hard time throwing the ball. I asked Barry if it would be alright if we went home, and he was more than fine with that.

At that time, the only reprieve from these symptoms was anti-inflammatories and Tylenol, so finding ways to relieve the pain required a lot of guesswork. Barry drew a warm bath for me to relax in while he made a soothing cup of herbal tea. When I was done with my bath, he was waiting with a warm terrycloth robe, floor-length Mickey Mouse style, fresh from the dryer. We cuddled on the couch and watched *Beauty And The Beast*.

Entertaining was a mainstay in our household. One evening when we had guests, I started having abdominal pains. Over the course of the evening, despite attempts to mitigate the pain, it continued to get worse. I excused myself and went to lie down. When Barry came to check on me, he made the call to take me to Emergency, despite the fact that we had guests.

At Emergency, we advised the nurses of the symptoms of my abdominal pain, and also mentioned that I had lupus. This seemed to cause a bit of alarm and I was admitted more quickly, but their reaction instilled us with panic. X-rays were taken immediately. When the doctor came to see us, in a loud voice, he asked when my last bowel movement had been. I really couldn't recall. Perhaps it had been a couple days. He responded by telling me that the problem was poop. Lots and lots of poop. I'm not one to get embarrassed, but I have to say I wanted so badly for him to stop talking about poop in this not-so-private room and in front of my fiancé. Offers were made to help the poop "flow," but all were graciously declined. I got a package of Exlax and returned home. This turned out to not be a symptom of my lupus, but thinking that it could have been made it scary enough.

My mother-in-law and I collected as much information as we could, which was surprisingly little back then. All I knew was that I was going to have to live with this, so I thought I had better learn how to deal with it. I needed to find out more. I couldn't be the only one with this disease. After locating a local lupus support group, I found out that there were thousands of us. Lupus is a chronic autoimmune disease that affects about fifty thousand Canadians, mostly women in their child-bearing years, but this disease really has no age or gender boundaries. With lupus, the immune system, which protects the body from germs, viruses, and bacteria, fails to distinguish between the body's own tissues and these foreign invaders. As a result, the immune system attacks different parts of the body, causing inflammation in those tissues.

I still remember the first support group I attended at the auditorium of a local hospital. Barry worked evenings, so his mom offered to take me. I probably never really thanked her for coming with me, but it meant a great deal to have my future mother-in-law at my side. I think this is when we really started to bond as a mother and daughter-in-law.

With all this happening, Barry and I felt it was important to continue the plans for our wedding. So, on May 9, 1992, I became Mrs. Christine Bonnett. This day was doubly special, as it was also my birthday. I can remember details about that day as though it was yesterday—all of the guests, the special dances, and how happy my husband looked, to name just a few. Barry still says it was the best party he's ever been to.

When I was diagnosed, the Lupus Society was quite small, with no real office space to speak of. It was run from a house in Carman, Manitoba. After attending an annual general meeting, I decided to become a board member. I took on the position of Vice-President and Director of Fundraising.

Trying to raise funds without a budget to work with was quite challenging at first. We started small, with craft and bake sales, usually held in the malls around the city.

I also had the lupus phone line installed in my home for a period of a year. This gave me one-on-one contact with new patients. They always had a million questions. As they told me, they felt comfortable speaking with someone who could relate to them. It also helped me, because I needed to remain positive in order to put them at ease.

Around this same time, I was also told I had hypothyroidism.[4] This is a condition in which the body lacks sufficient thyroid hormone. Symptoms may vary from mild

---

4 Hypothyroidism: "Diminished production of thyroid hormone , leading to clinical manifestations of thyroid insufficiency, including sommolence, slow mentation, dryness and loss of hair, subnormal temperature, hoarseness, muscle weakness, delayed relaxation of tender reflexes and sometimes myxederma." (from *Stedman's Medical Dictionary for the Health Professions and Nursing, Illustrated Fifth Edition* [Baltimore, MD: Lippincott, Williams and Wilkins, 2005], 713).

to severe and from non-specific to very specific. In general, all metabolic processes slow down. Patients are often fatigued and may also have depression, decreased intellectual function, and (rarely) overt psychosis. Patients frequently complain of cold intolerance, dry skin, and constipation. The heart rate is often slowed, as is the relaxation phase of deep tendon reflexes. This is a very common medical condition. In fact, as many as ten percent of women may unknowingly have some degree of thyroid hormone deficiency. This can be determined by a simple blood test. Hypothyroidism can be hereditary. My dad and two of my brothers live with this condition.

With all of this happening to my body, and not knowing the outcome, Barry and I had some decisions to make. The decision not to have children was not easy to make. Growing up, I always saw myself being a mother one day. After consulting with a number of doctors and family members, it was suggested that we not have children. There are millions of women living with lupus who choose to have children. At the time, we felt the risk would be too great for me. The decision may have been different if I had been the healthy spouse.

I didn't realize how difficult it would be to live with that choice. For the first while, it was hard to even see a mother with her newborn. My close friends were having children. They were all aware of my situation and I think they felt they had to tiptoe around me on the subject of children. I hope I made it clear that I wanted to share all aspects of their lives, and having a child is a big part. All I asked was that they cherish what they had been given and be the best parents they could be.

To help fill the void, I spent a considerable amount of time with my nephew and nieces, and I still try to today. I have three nieces who live in Winnipeg (Danna, Ayla, Chloe), and one niece in Ottawa (Sophie). My nephew lives in Guelph (Danny). On Barry's side of the family I also have a niece and nephews who I don't see as often as I'd like (Gordon, Alicia, Connor, and Cameron),

Chloe, Ayla, and Danna enjoy a Christmas snuggle with Auntie Chris

Auntie Chris and Sophie on her 4th birthday

which I hope changes one day. At present they all range in ages from twelve to thirty-three years. When they were growing up, I really tried hard not to miss a birthday or special event in their lives. I admit that we went a little crazy at Christmas, as far as gifts go, but wasn't that our job as an aunt and uncle?

It had been so exciting to watch my brothers grow up to become amazing and caring fathers. I couldn't wait to see what paths my nieces and nephew travelled on. I hoped to always be a part of their lives. I tried to keep the lines of communication open, so if they needed to talk about something they could come to me. I hoped they knew that our door would always be open for them.

I cannot end the chapter without mentioning the two cutest American Cocker Spaniels you ever did see. I'm pretty sure we moved into a house just so we could get a dog. When we went to pick up the pup, there were only two of the litter left. We just couldn't take one and leave the other alone. That's how we ended up with Gozer and

Merlin. Although they're both gone now, I'm still amazed at how they always knew when I needed an extra cuddle.

4.

DAD

"Daddy's Little Girl" (Al Martino)

In 1995, my dad was diagnosed with emphysema.[5]

During this time, I also received a call from someone telling me that my oldest brother Norm had suffered a hockey accident. I didn't think much of it in the moment because he had numerous hockey bumps and bruises. However, I started to worry when I couldn't get a hold of him or his wife.

---

5 "a condition of the lung characterized by increase beyond the normal in the size of the air spaces distal to the terminal brochiole (those parts containing alveoli), with destructive changes in their walls and reduction in their number" (from *Stedman's Medical Dictionary for the Health Professions and Nursing, Illustrated Fifth Edition* [Baltimore, MD: Lippincott, Williams and Wilkins, 2005], 468).

After a few calls to his friends, I found out he was at a hospital in the eye clinic, but I didn't know his status. The hospital wouldn't give me any information over the phone. What was I to do?

Mom was visiting Dad at a different hospital, so I went to be with them for a while. I told one of the nurses there about Norm and she offered to call the other hospital to talk to his nurse. Well, as soon as I heard that he was having surgery, I made excuses and went straight to the eye clinic. I didn't tell Mom Dad, not wanting to worry them until I had the all the facts.

I met my sister-in-law Sharon in the hospital ward. She told me he had been hit in his left eye with a puck, and there was no chance of saving the eye. He came out of surgery and was okay—or at least as well as you can be when you've lost an eye. I left to let him sleep a while.

I remember driving home to an empty house. Barry was working, my brothers Jack and Dan were on a fishing trip, Mom was with Dad, and my brother Scot was

Me with my brother Norm on his wedding day, 1978 (left), and on my own wedding day, 1992 (right)

overseas. I needed to talk to someone, so I called Scot in China and didn't care about the phone bill. I just needed to hear a familiar voice. I needed him to tell me Norm would be alright, that he would bounce right back. Norm did recover and was back to work and driving in no time. To this day, I have a renewed respect for him and the way he coped.

On July 15, 1997, I received a call at work that Dad had been taken to the hospital and that I should get there asap. Dad was in a coma by the time I arrived. This was my first time seeing someone in a coma. I wanted to believe that he was just having a good sleep and was in no pain at all. He had a number of visitors, including a priest to perform the last rites. We all held hands and stood around his bed, praying. The doctors said he could remain in his coma for days. We wanted to make sure he was never alone, so we all took shifts staying with him.

Scot and I stayed the first night. His room was right next to the lounge and I would try to get a little shuteye there. The nurses were just super to us, offering coffee and pillows. The next night, Jack and Dan stayed. It was around 2:00 a.m. when Dad passed away, with Jack and Dan on either side of him. It was somewhat comforting to know he was not alone in that last hour.

We all came to the hospital. I'm not sure why we all went, but it was just something we felt we needed to do. We all stood around his bed in silence. Our family wasn't used to silence, which says just how taken aback we were with this experience. This death was different than that of our grandparents, or even a close family friend. This was our dad! We knew from that moment on that our lives would be changed forever.

When we finally started to walk out, a nurse came to us with a set of false teeth. Scot grabbed them and put them in his pocket. Mom was quite upset, saying something about how "we don't need those." We were thinking she meant that since he was gone he wouldn't be needing his teeth. Nothing else was said about it that night. The next morning, we all met at Mom's to discuss funeral arrangements. I was in charge of picking out a suit and tie for Dad. Suddenly, she asked that someone clean his teeth before we headed off to the funeral home. Scot jumped up, grabbed the teeth from his pocket, cleaned them, and put them in a bag by the door. About ten minutes later, Mom walked in with a set of teeth asking why nobody had cleaned them. Scot insisted that he *had* cleaned them. Mom said, "Well, they don't look clean to me." Scot then realized that the container Mom was holding

Dad and me; Easter, 1984

was different from the one he had cleaned and put in the bag. I can still remember the scream I heard from Scot when he realized that the hospital had given us someone else's teeth. We all just lost it—with laughter, I mean. We were almost giddy, since none of us had had much sleep in the past few days. We badly needed a good laugh. Mom wanted to believe that Dad had had something to do with the mix up, as he had always been quite the joker. Scot returned the teeth to the hospital. The nurses were sincere about the confusion, but there was a great embarrassed roar of laughter when he walked away.

Growing up, my dad used a lot of colourful metaphors. One of the most memorable of these came when I was eight years old and had a couple of girlfriends stay for a sleepover. We were all sitting at the breakfast table when my dad asked, in his most gruff voice, to have the "baby shit" passed to him. The looks of horror and disbelief on my friends' faces were priceless. As they watched, I casually passed my father the "baby shit," otherwise known as peanut butter. My father had strange nicknames for all sorts of everyday things. My friends were onto the game when he asked for the cow and gravel to put into his coffee (milk and sugar).

As Daddy's little girl, I'm still dealing with his loss in my life. I still want to call him when I see a western or police drama on TV that he would have loved to see. He was always ready to give advice on a car or house repair. From what I've heard from talking to family and friends, these feelings are quite normal. However, that doesn't change how much I miss him.

5.

DIAGNOSIS—OPTIC NEURITIS

"These Eyes" (The Guess Who)

A few years went by with little incident, medically speaking. My lupus seemed to be in remission. The year 1999, however, would be the start of another downward spiral. First came the headaches. Then I noticed my left eye drooping. My doctor set up an appointment with a neurologist. This appointment resulted in another diagnosis.

In the summer of 2000, I was diagnosed with myasthenia gravis (MG),[6] a disease in

---

6 "Myasthenia gravis is a neuromuscular disorder primarily characterized by muscle weakness and muscle fatigue. Although the disorder usually becomes apparent during adulthood, symptom onset may occur at any age. The condition

which muscles are quickly fatigued from repetitive use. Myasthenia gravis is characterized by detrimental neuronal response with repetitive nerve stimulation and evidences itself in a few characteristic ways. It is typical for a myasthenic patient to have a flattened smile and droopy eyes, with slow pupillary light responses. The patient may have fixed column deformity or irregular posture after standing for a short period of time. Nasal speech, difficulty chewing and swallowing, and dulled facial expression (including difficulty smiling and an ineffective cough due to weak expiratory muscles) are frequently associated with MG.

On October 15, 2001, I had a thymectomy. This is the removal of the thymus gland, one which most of us have never even heard

---

may be restricted to certain muscle groups, particularly those of the eyes (ocular myasthenia gravis), or may become more generalized (generalized myasthenia gravis), involving multiple muscle groups" (from "Myasthenia Gravis," *WebMD*, September 17, 2013 [http://www.webmd.com/a-to-z-guides/myasthenia-gravis-10819]).

of. My doctors had made a link between this gland and MG. They also had clinical proof that removing the gland could result in an improvement in the stages of MG. Since my body was rejecting the suggested medications, this procedure was recommended.

A month later, I woke up with an enormous headache and no vision in my left eye. I was absolutely stunned. I started the morning in my neurologist's office. He sent me to an ophthalmologist who specialized in corneas, then to another ophthalmologist who specialized in retinas. It was this doctor who diagnosed me with optic neuritis. This is when the optic nerve becomes inflamed and doesn't allow light to pass through. Armed with a diagnosis, I returned to my neurologist's office. He was the one who was supposed to explain what the hell we were dealing with. (Did I mention that I was able to see all these specialists in one morning? I have never complained about the medical attention I have received thus far.) He basically told Barry and me that we had two choices: do nothing and let the condition take its course or get five days of intravenous steroid treatments to help reduce the swelling of the optic nerve, which could also ease some of the pain. I chose the steroids, a decision I'm sure many would have made. I felt it was better than doing nothing.

After the fifth treatment, the pain subsided and I regained some of the vision in that eye. It was likely this would happen again, and each time it happened I was to expect less vision to return. So I wasn't surprised when it happened again at the end of January 2002. I went through the same procedure as before—five days of steroids, hoping for the best. At this time, my brother Dan was in the same hospital. I was allowed to walk around while I was getting my treatments. I would walk up to his room to keep him company. Dan also lived with a chronic autoimmune illness. He had been diagnosed with common variable agammaglobulin anemia,[7] an immune dysfunction

---

7 "Anemia is a condition that develops when your blood lacks enough healthy red blood cells. These cells are the main

by which no antibodies were able to attach to his B-cells to fight off infections. This disease would cause a variety of health-related complications throughout his life. Even though he was hospitalized for weeks and in a worse condition than I was, he was always so worried about me. A typical big brother reaction. I was the only girl and would always be the baby of the family in my older brothers' eyes. I was and still am well watched over.

Even after the steroids, I discovered I had lost vision in that one eye completely. Where was I to go from here? Well, onward of course! Remember, I had my brother Norm as an example of someone who lived quite normally with one eye. I tried wearing a patch for a while, but the headaches were

---

transporters of oxygen to organs. If red blood cells are also deficient in hemoglobin, then your body isn't getting enough oxygen. Symptoms of anemia—like fatigue—occur because organs aren't getting what they need to function properly" (from "Understanding Anemia—the Basics," *WebMD*, September 17, 2013 [http://www.webmd.com/a-to-z-guides/understanding-anemia-basics]).

too frequent. Dealing with this transition was still trying at times. All I saw was a big white fluffy cloud, which interfered with the vision of my right eye.

Throughout all this, I continued to work fulltime, except for days on which I needed to go in for steroid treatments. I felt I couldn't be entirely truthful with my employers about my condition, for fear of losing my job. But what was there to be truthful about? I still had no idea where this nightmare was headed. So I went on as if it had no real impact on me and my daily routine.

6.

Hospital Stays

"I Wanna Be Sedated" (The Ramones)

March 2002 came along and reminded me of just how fragile our bodies can be. This time, I knew the vision loss was coming. I started having headaches a few days prior and the sight in my right eye was slowly deteriorating until March 11, when I woke and had no vision at all. I can't even begin to explain how terrified I was. I was trying to keep my husband calm while I casually mentioned to him that we needed to get to my neurologist's office as soon as possible. At least that's the way I remember that morning. His recollection may be completely different.

When I called the neurologist's office, he wanted me to get to an ophthalmologist's office so they could take a look at the entire eye. I was squeezed into one doctor's schedule and he confirmed what we already knew: my vision was further deteriorating. I then went to my neurologist's office and was told that he was at the hospital. It was his day to work in Emergency.

As fate would have it, we were on our way to that same hospital to visit Dan. We let the doctor's receptionist know where we were. After a half-hour, my doctor came right to Dan's room to collect me and shuffle me off to the doctors' lounge. He consulted with three or four other doctors about my situation. They were all mystified. They didn't know if this was related to my lupus or something totally new, possibly MS. They agreed to admit me right then and there. The tests started—CT scans, MRIs, X-rays, and plenty of blood work. They gave me the highest dose of steroids I had ever been on. I swear, you could have put down a horse with the amount I was given.

I was in a semi-private room and had the bed closest to the window, which also meant furthest from the bathroom. My bathroom trips were okay as long as I had friends and family there to help. However, I'll never forget the first time I had to call a staff member to assist me in going to the washroom. My roommate was unable to assist me, as she was a ninety-year-old woman who only spoke French. It was in the middle of the night and a female staff member answered my call bell. I could hear her sighs. I could have sworn she was rolling her eyes. She grabbed my wrist without letting me know she was about to touch me and proceeded to drag me to the washroom. She positioned me between the toilet and herself, spun me around, and backed me up until the backs of my knees hit the toilet. She pulled my underwear down and then, with her hands on my shoulders, pushed me down until I was seated on the toilet.

    She handed me a cord and told me to pull it when I was done, and then she walked out. I started to cry because I thought this was what the rest of my life was going to hold for me.

As the week progressed, I started to feel braver and attempted to walk to the bathroom on my own. In doing so, I would have to hold on to the wall and my roommate's bed. Even the staff was finding it difficult to communicate with her, as very few of them spoke French. One day, my friend Gail, who speaks French, came to visit. Before I even let her take her coat off, I asked her to speak to my roommate and see if there was anything she needed. What she had been trying to communicate to the staff was that her cane was nowhere to be found. It had been with her in Emergency and she wanted to make sure it wasn't lost. Gail relayed the message to the nursing station and they were more than happy to go and look for it. I then asked Gail to let my roommate know why I was in the hospital.

My roommate gasped as she realized her mistake. She had thought I was drunk from the way I staggered to the bathroom.

Another memorable incident occurred when a healthcare aide came in and asked if I was hungry, to which I answered, "Yes, I am!"

"Why didn't you touch your food tray?" she asked.

"What food tray?"

"The food tray right there."

Again I said, "What food tray?"

I can only assume she was pointing to a food tray. Nobody had told me it was there when they dropped it off, and I certainly couldn't see it.

I feel the need to share my first shower experience as a blind person while in the hospital. A male healthcare aide came in to tell me he was there to give me a sponge bath, to which I replied, "Hell no!" We argued back and forth for a bit. My argument was that my body parts hadn't moved overnight and I still knew where they were. I didn't need assistance. I ended up calling the charge nurse, who agreed with me, that all I needed was someone to guide me to and from the shower room.

Barry was there to help me with my next shower. Once I was starting to get undressed in the shower room, I heard Barry say, "Chris, can you handle anything more?"

When I asked what he was referring to, he had to let me know something that most husbands would never usually speak of—I had started my period. I sighed, saying, "Well, I'm going to continue getting them, so why not now?"

Wow! In those few days, I learned a lot about how difficult some tasks are for a blind person, tasks that a sighted person would take for granted.

My hospital stay was unique. I didn't feel ill; it's just that they had no idea why I had lost my vision. They wanted me in the hospital to perform various tests. I really didn't mind being in the hospital, because I figured that as long as I was there, they were still looking for a cause. I also didn't mind because Dan was in the hospital on a different floor. He would come to visit me and I would do the same in return. We would help each other take our minds off our situations for a while. All the nurses on Dan's floor knew about my case, but not from the doctors. Dan would tell them how worried he was about me. It was only fair, I guess, since

I was equally worried about his situation, which was much more serious than mine.

7.

THE BREAK-IN

"Alone" (Heart)

Because I was virtually blind, I was unable to work, so I was put on short-term disability until we could figure out what needed to be done.

After a full week at the hospital, I was happy about getting home. Or was I? Barry worked midnights, which meant he needed to sleep during the day. When you cannot see, there isn't a lot you can do during the day. For the first little while I couldn't cook, so I had to wait until Barry woke up to make us supper. I was scared to even go outside by myself for fear of walking into something. I really was not prepared for a life of darkness. I thought it would be a piece of cake, but instead I was confronted with many obstacles. I couldn't drive anymore, so a large part of my independence was instantly gone. I had to ask my husband to help me with little things like my styling my hair and dressing. I could dress myself, but I needed him let me know if I looked like a complete idiot before leaving the house. I could understand how someone might become agoraphobic. I found myself making excuses not to leave the house unless someone was with me. I hated these new feelings of insecurity, which I wasn't used to. Since I had no idea when or if my vision would return, I needed to nip this feeling in the bud.

The first evening I went out was with Barry and our friends Rob and Denika. We all bowled in a league. Obviously I didn't go to bowl, but just to get out and be around people. After the bowling ended, Barry headed directly to work and Rob and Denika drove me home. When we arrived at my house, Denika was kind enough to walk me to the door. I'm so glad she did, because as we went to put the key in the door, we noticed that the door was open. We'd had a break-in!

I couldn't believe it. After checking to make sure the dogs were safe, I called the police. Before the police arrived, I also called Barry and asked him to come home, as I was frightened to stay alone. I couldn't help thinking what would have happened if I'd been home alone when they broke in. I tried to stay away from that kind of thinking.

The following week, we had an alarm system installed, by Oakley Alarms. Actually, my brother Norm and his wife Sharon paid for the alarm to be installed and monitored for three years. With me on disability, they knew money was tight. Sometimes I am in awe of just how supportive my family is. Statistics show that a large majority of people get systems after their first break-in. I guess we were no different.

As though I wasn't already going through enough, now I added to the list a feeling vulnerable in my own home. For months afterwards, every little noise made me jump. It took me a long while to feel comfortable again.

8.

DAN

"Cat's In The Cradle" (Harry Chapin)

April brought heart-breaking news. Dan's disease was getting the better of him. For the first time, I was happy to be off work. This meant I had much more time to spend with my brother and his family in his last days. We had some good one-on-one talks which I will always cherish.

Dan was eleven years older than me. During one of his hospital stays, I was visiting on my own. For once he had no other visitors, so I had him all to myself. He was feeling a bit down this day and talking about the burden he believed he had become to his wife and family. You would think that a sister would offer a hug, but I'm not like most sisters, so I slapped him upside the head and reminded him of the legacy he'd be leaving this earth. He had great kids and an amazing wife who admired and respected him. Thinking back, I can't believe I actually had that conversation with him. I grew up idolizing all my brothers, so telling him off was out of character for me.

I would visit Dan as often as I could when he went to the hospital's cancer care treatment centre. Part of his treatment involved intravenous steroids. If anyone has had steroids, you know all too well that steroids give you a boost to your appetite. The hospital had wonderful volunteers who went around with little carts of coffee, tea and cookies. At first I would go out to the hallway and get Dan a couple cookies and maybe tea. That wouldn't be enough, however, so I'd get another couple of cookies, and another, until he said, "Screw it. Bring in the whole tray."

I felt like a bank robber. I'd look around to see that nobody was looking and then grab the tray with all the cookies and he'd chow down. And this was before lunch! For lunch, I'd go to a nearby drive-in and get him a burger, fries, and shake. It was amazing because, he never had that kind of appetite at home. I loved watching him eat.

My niece Danna started accompanying her dad to his "juice-ups" at a young age—that's the nickname we used for his treatments. Many of my nieces and nephews are now regular blood donors for Canadian Blood Services. Dan would be proud of them, as am I.

He tried to stay as connected as possible with his little sister. During my high school years, he coached the boys' basketball team, and he even dared to coach our girls' baseball team for a couple of seasons. For those of you who are wondering, yes, he was harder on me than anyone else. In the end, I think it made me a better player. Dan also took me to my very first live rock concert. It was Loverboy in 1982 at the Winnipeg Arena. I had no idea what to expect, or what was expected of me. People were standing and dancing all around me, including my brother. I remember him looking at me like I had two heads because I wasn't joining in at first. Eventually I stood up and got into it!

Dan and his family, along with my sister-in law Sabrina and nieces Ayla and Chloe, religiously attended our city's Folk Festival for years. I have heard wonderful stories, but I could never go because of my lupus (I couldn't sit out in the sun). They would tell me about the awesome music, buy me a CD of somebody they thought I would like, and tell me about the day and how wonderful it had been.

I finally got to go in 2011 on a day when KD Lang was performing. When she sang "Hallelujah," I wept. I have never been brought to tears by a performance before, but I think it was a combination of things. Maybe it was because I was on Dan's turf and he wasn't there. The music was so beautiful; she hit every note perfectly. I was outside enjoying the fresh air with the thousands of other people all there for the same reason. It was so exhilarating! I hope to go again someday.

Dan and Me

Dan knew he was terminal and decisions had to be made in respect to palliative care. I went to the hospital with his family, where he filled out the paperwork for him to be added to the waiting list. Dan thanked me for coming with them that afternoon. All I could say was that he didn't have to thank me. I knew that if our roles had been reversed, he would have been there for me in a heartbeat.

I only hope he knew how much he was loved and would be missed. His last days were sad, but also touching. Sitting with the family, we spoke of our amazing times together. Even then, we would say, "If Dan could hear us, he would kick our asses for crying instead of celebrating his life!" We did try to celebrate his life, and what a life it was!

To this day, his funeral was the best funeral I've ever been to. I have never heard so much laughter, and that's exactly the way he would have wanted it. I know I'm being selfish when I say I wish he was still here to talk to—usually about health-related issues. He was the only one in my life who could truly relate with, and who understood how I was feeling.

9.

The Middle East

"You've Got A Friend" (James Taylor)

After all this, I was finally looking forward to something. Near the end of June 2002, I would be traveling overseas for the first time. By this time, I had regained a good percentage of vision in my right eye; I was still blind in the left. I was excited and terrified all at once, as I would be traveling by myself.

My brother Scot and his wife Donica were in the diplomatic corps and were serving in Jordan. Scot took time off to meet me in Austria. The airlines were wonderful to me. I was escorted to all my gates and waiting points. Scot and I packed quite a bit into our few days in Austria. We made sure to see Vienna, then Salzburg. Our stay

Scot, Sophie and me at the Cave Bar in Petra, Jordan

in Vienna included a Mozart concert in the most spectacular concert hall I had ever seen. I had a lot of firsts there—the first time on a train, a subway and a streetcar. After our sightseeing in Austria was over, we jumped on a plane and headed to Amman, Jordan.

Donica was *charge d'affaire* (acting ambassador). When I was there, we used the flag car—the ambassador's—to go to a reception at the British Embassy. I had the opportunity to float in the Dead Sea, get an authentic Turkish bath, see Petra (where one of Indiana Jones movies was filmed), and stay one night for shopping in Damascus, Syria.

The other reason I was there was to see my youngest niece, Sophie. It was refreshing to watch a three-year-old experience life. She was full of life and made me laugh. I appreciated her simple outlook. That was a trip of a lifetime and I'll be eternally grateful to Scot and Donica for making it happen.

When I arrived home—and after seeing doctor after doctor and taking test after test, all with no results—I was physically and mentally exhausted.

10.

Back To Work

"9–5" (Dolly Parton)

With no doctors able to give me answers. I needed to feel like something was being done. I contacted the Canadian Institute for the Blind (CNIB) to inquire about their services.

By this time, I had regained a considerable amount of vision in my right eye. I had come to terms with the fact that my left eye was gone for good. What did this mean? Could I go back to work? My insurance company put me in touch with an occupational therapist, and together we devised a rehab plan for me to return to work. It took four to five months to get everything in order, but it was well worth the wait. With the help of CNIB, I was able to get some equipment from the Vocational Rehab Program of Manitoba to help me at my desk, including a twenty-two-inch monitor, large print keyboard, and enhancing software called Zoom Text.

In November 2002, I went back to work for half days. I was excited about being back and felt happy to be useful again. By the beginning of January, I was back full-time and in the groove again.

In the afternoon of January 17, 2003, Barry came to see me at work. His Nana had been rushed to the hospital after having a heart attack in the night. The doctors suspected she would not make it through the day. With this news, I left work with Barry. A few hours later, she very peacefully passed away with her family at her side. My mother-in-law asked me to do the eulogy at the funeral. I was honoured that she would ask me. I was used to public speaking, but this was a unique circumstance, as I would be retelling someone's life. Barry and I sat up for two nights writing and rewriting. We tried our best to do her credit; she had been a sweet woman with a strong will. It was an intimate service with family and close friends.

Near the end of January, I was feeling quite drained. I wasn't sure if it because of my lack of vision or the large workload. Was it too much for me to take on so soon? Who could say? Extra money was found in our department budget to hire another person to work with me. Relief was near! Thank God! When this person started in February, I could feel the weight being lifted off my shoulders. I was much more relaxed, and I'm sure everyone in my life could tell.

11.

British Isles

"Consequence Free" (Great Big Sea)

In 2005, we were lucky enough to put some money away to take a trip to England, where Barry had some relatives. Unfortunately, I lost my sight just before we went, so I did not see a lot of England. I still enjoyed all the sounds and smells and tastes, though, not to mention meeting so many new people. It was incredible! After our wonderful time in England, we flew to Aberdeen, Scotland, where we met up with my brothers Jack, Norm and his wife Sharon, Scot and his wife Donica, and my niece Sophie. We all stayed in a town called Cruden Bay, where our Grandpa Slessor had lived. I can't explain what it was like to walk down roads that our grandfather had walked

Norm, Jack, Scot, and Me sharing a pint in Cruden Bay, Scotland, 2005

down as a child. Also, as our plane touched down in Scotland, I regained a large portion of the vision in my right eye. This was amazing; it meant I would be able to see Scotland. Everything was beautiful, and the people were wonderful and friendly.

I know we all felt a tinge of guilt, because Dan would have loved to be there. For most of his life, he had talked about Scotland and wanting to go there. Unfortunately, he had been too sick to ever make the trip.

Now, here we were, doing what he could never do.

We had a drink for Dan in one of the pubs.

12.

AND THEN THERE WERE FOUR

"Que Sera Sera" (Doris Day)

The roller coaster ride was about to begin all over again, however. On the last Sunday in March, I received a phone call from my brother Jack. He was calling from our mom's house, informing me that he had found her lying on the floor in the hallway, and that I should get over there as soon as I could. I woke Barry up.

As we drove up to the house, we saw that the paramedics were already there. I will never forget how terrified Mom looked as the paramedics worked on her. She had fallen and was too weak to get up. We really had no idea how long she had been lying there all alone. I drove with Mom in the ambulance and felt like I wasn't really there... she was in a kind of dream-like state. This didn't feel real, but it was *very* real. This was happening.

When we arrived at the hospital, I gave all my mom's medical information to the nurse at the emergency desk. After moving her into observation, they realized right away that she was dehydrated, so they started an intravenous. Next came the battery of testing, X-rays, and CT scans to see if any damage had been done as a result of her fall. She had no broken bones, but they suspected she'd had a stroke. Later in the week, she was diagnosed with having celiac.[8]

At least we had a diagnosis, something we could wrap our heads around. This was a workable situation. We thought that if we could help alter her diet, everything would

---

8 Celiac disease: "a disease occurring in children and adults characterized by sensitivity to gluten, with chronic inflammation and atrophy of the mucosa of the upper small intestine; manifestations include diarrhea, malabsorption, steatorrhea and nutritional and vitamin deficiencies" (from *Stedman's Medical Dictionary for the Health Professions and Nursing, Illustrated Fifth Edition* [Baltimore, MD: Lippincott, Williams and Wilkins, 2005], 250).

be alright. Unfortunately, that wasn't even close to true.

After a week of having both good days and bad days, Sunday came and she was very alert. She knew we were all there, even thanking her grandchildren for coming to visit. We all went home feeling good.

At 5:00 a.m., I was woken up by the doorbell. It was my brother Scot, telling me that the hospital had called and suggested we all come down as soon as possible. That same dream-like feeling came over me again as I quickly dressed and rushed out the door with him.

When we arrived at the hospital, she was already in a coma. She'd had a heart attack during the night and was just too weak to fight it. We were told it was only a matter of time. I was so shocked, I couldn't even cry. I don't think I had any emotion. Throughout the day, Mom had a number of visitors wanting to say farewell. Then, at about 10:00 p.m., as I was at her side, holding her hand, she fell into a deep sleep surrounded by her four surviving children and Barry.

Mom and me enjoying a family celebration

At the risk of sounding a little corny, when we sold my childhood home after that, I felt like a part of me went with the house. My mother was the main reason our house was a home. Everyone on our block knew that my mom had been known as the cookie lady. At any given time, my friends knew there was a steady supply of homemade cookies in our kitchen. She was also a card shark, but only at crib; if the game was poker, her face would give away what she had in her hand. My mom also had the ability to stretch a dollar, a skill she unfortunately did not pass on to me. I'm still amazed at how she kept clothes on our backs and food in our mouths with the small amount of money that came in.

When we first moved into the house, there were seven of us, and only four of us were there to sell it. The impact of selling the house was a blow I wasn't ready for. I realized it was just a house, but the memories made it a home. It was compounded by the deaths of Dad, Dan, and now Mom. It hit me like a brick. The loss was inconceivable.

13.

Going Blind

"I Go Blind" (54-40)

After many doctors, treatments, and medications, the inevitable happened in June 2006. Ever since then, I have lived with absolutely no vision. I knew this could happen, but nothing you tell yourself can ever really prepare you for a life of darkness.

When something so traumatic happens, the troops rally and help where they are able. Slowly, however, that support thins until you find yourself somewhat alone. "That's just life," I kept telling myself. I had to learn—or should I say, relearn—basic life skills.

Indeed, following my last bout of optic neuritis, I was told I was completely blind.

This forced me to call on CNIB for new training, as what I knew to date would serve me little. Mobility was (and still remains) the most challenging transition. I feel the need to emphasize that even having a sliver of sight can make a world of difference as opposed to being completely blind.

How do I describe the experience of becoming blind? Losing your sight is surreal and traumatic. I had known this last episode was coming and just had a feeling that it would be the last of my sight. I had woken up before with no vision, but this time it was different, because the odds of any sight returning were not in my favour.

Unfortunately, like anyone who experiences trauma, I initially concentrated on the negative side of things. For me, I thought about never again being able to see the face of my husband, or never being able to see my nieces in their graduation or wedding gowns. Those frustrations will never go away, so I have to face them. I just have to deal with it, I suppose. I can't change it.

I was still looking for the reason this happened to me. Was this meant to be? What purpose could this have? Was I supposed to go out and advocate for all blind and visually impaired folks? Was I not humble enough?

As you could well imagine, many days I wondered why the hell I was even still alive. I would be lying if I said I never thought life would be easier for all those around me if I simply wasn't there. Then I would think, *if I die today, what kind of legacy would I leave?* My answer was always, "Not much."

In the months that followed, I met a lot of incredible people who lived with vision loss. I was nowhere near their league. I couldn't even be a good blind person. I felt like I was sucking the life and money out of my husband, and even the government, since I had to rely on disability insurance.

I had no idea that people would react the way they did. I was ignored in stores and restaurants. I understood that they are uncomfortable, but I could also understand how people with disabilities grow to be less tolerant of the ignorant people they meet up with.

I have been a speaker for the United Way. I would speak to employers and their staffs about my personal story and how the United Way had impacted my life.

I probably could have handled the transition better if it hadn't been for the loneliness. The feeling of isolation was indescribable. I really felt that if I never picked up the phone, I would never hear from anyone ever again. Maybe this was what supposed to happen to me. My family got together and bought me the software I needed in order to get on the computer again. I really was appreciative, but I wondered what my family and friends would say if they knew how much more it would mean to me just to go for the occasional coffee or bite to eat.

This held true for Barry also. I had put him through a lot and a man can only handle so much. I wasn't sure if he was as comfortable with all this as he said and thought he was. I could never tell him just how lonely and depressed I had become.

I knew he loved and cared for me, but what was I to expect? It was amazing how many people in my life told me how lucky I was to have him. But I knew that! I wonder if people were thinking he was also lucky to have me.

I wasn't alone in having these feelings of hopelessness and despair. I can't speak for everybody, and I wouldn't want to, but I've spoken to a number of people who have a variety of disabilities, and there are some commonalities.

I can speak to the vision loss, because I have been a co-facilitator for a support group called "Transitions" at CNIB for seven years. It's a wonderful way to give back, not to mention a good way to get out and keep busy. Sometimes, however, I almost feel like I'm a fraud. Here I am, trying to help people who have lost their vision and they're trying to deal with it the best way they can. They have a lot of questions, emotions are raw, and I don't know if I've even dealt with this myself—not completely. It's kind of ironic, but we muddle through each session together.

I can speak about having multiple disabilities. In addition to losing my sight, I have a mobility issue - which comes up a bit later. I can't use my left hand, so I can't read braille. Typing on a computer is not an easy task for me, so getting a job has been difficult.

When you become blind, you treat it as a loss. You go into a period of grieving, because there are many losses that come with it. Losing your driver's license is a biggie, because that means losing independence, losing control in your life, confidence, security about who you are, and self-worth. A whole realm of insecurities emerge because you don't feel you can contribute to your family the way you used to. You start to feel like you're becoming a burden. One hears that word all the time, but I say it because I feel it; other people say it because they feel it. I wish there was a nicer word, but unfortunately there isn't.

Weird things started to happen soon after my vision loss. For the most part, people were helpful, but sometimes they were not so helpful. Here are some of my pet peeves (which are common among people with vision loss):

> People talking louder and slower to me.
>
> People, specifically in the service industry (waiters, cashiers, etc.), speaking to the person or people I'm with instead of me regarding my order or purchase.
>
> People grabbing my arm without telling me they are going to do so.
>
> People telling me we are approaching stairs, but neglect to say whether we are going up or down.

It wasn't just me who had to learn to deal with what happened; it was everyone I came in contact with, whether personal or professional. I had to trust people to do the right thing when helping me—service people, friends, even family. I don't think the word "vulnerable" even scratches the surface of how at the mercy of other people a blind person can be.

Hospital Roommates (names changed)

I spent a total of nine and half months in hospitals. During these stays, I had the esteemed honour of meeting a number of roommates. The first word that comes to mind when describing the diverse collection of my multiple roommates is "Wow."

I can still hear Mr. Brown across the hall at the first hospital, yelling for someone to bring his car around. After shouting this command at least three times with no response, he proceeded to start firing the hired help (nursing staff) on the spot. Back in his day, I suspect Mr. Brown had been the CEO executive type.

Miss Ruby, another roommate at the first hospital, was in her eighties and suffered from dementia. When her daughter and husband came to visit, she would respond to them by smiling. One day, she was having a particularly awful day trying to communicate with hospital staff. Out of sheer frustration, utensils started flying in my general direction. I don't believe she was actually trying to maim me, but obviously something needed to be done, for my safety.

Sister White was a new roommate who did not speak English. She made it clear, however, that she enjoyed her brandy.

Another roommate was known as the "drill sergeant." She had been in the army back in the day and was used to giving orders. When my family or friends weren't around, she became my protector and would tell the staff to look after me.

Being alone with people you don't know and cannot see evokes feelings that are hard to describe. I can hear when they move in and out of the room, or up and down the hall. Unless they worked with me directly, most of the hospital staff—and, of course, all the patients on the floor—were unaware that I was blind.

14.

Romance In The Yukon

"Somewhere Over The Rainbow"
(Izrael "Iz" Kamakawiwo'ole)

Travelling to my nephew Danny's wedding in the Yukon was to be my first air travel after going completely blind. Barry couldn't go with me because he was unable to get the time off work. Instead I went with my brothers Jack and Norm, my sister in-law Sharon, and my niece Ayla. I felt pretty secure and comfortable having my family with me. Sharon worked with the airlines, so we were able to get first-class seats for at least a couple of us, which was wonderful.

We arrived safely in the Yukon from Winnipeg. The wedding was wonderful! We got to meet my nephew Danny's in-laws. Coincidentally, his new wife Kelly had two aunts who are visually impaired, and they

Danny and Kelly's wedding, 2006

were also attending the wedding. This was a small wedding, with perhaps thirty guests in total, and three of us were visually impaired! What are the odds?

During the reception, Danny and Kelly wanted the guests to sing, tell a joke, or do something silly to get the couple to *kiss.* I got the visually-impaired aunts together and we sang "Three Blind Mice." It was hilarious and everyone enjoyed it.

Kelly's family was so down to earth, it was like sitting down with old friends. It was a wonderful day and a wonderful wedding. We took a daytrip to Alaska and had a superb time! I couldn't even be upset at the fact that I was blind and couldn't see anything. My nieces and brothers and sisters-in-law were doing their best to include me in everything and describe everything around us, making sure I wasn't alone. They were absolutely wonderful.

Looking back, not only was this my first time travelling after I completely lost my sight, but it was also my first opportunity to dance. I love dancing—and music. I couldn't lose the opportunity to dance, so I found someone from my family help me to the dance floor. Once I started moving to the music, I drifted away from the people I was dancing with. My equilibrium was off. I would start turning around, and sometimes my back would be to the group. Oh my word! But my family would very casually turn me around. It was cool. I was embarrassed for maybe a second each time, but it was with family so it was okay. What can I say? Love was in the air, so it was all positive and light and fluffy and everybody was in a great mood. Everybody was happy. The weather was great, too.

15.

Radio Show

"I Did It My Way" (Paul Anka)

In 2007, my brother Jack and I decided to embark on a fundraising project together. This event would take the shape of an old-time radio show. We called it "The Golden Days of Canadian Radio." All proceeds were to be donated to CNIB.

Jack produced the commercials and cheesy show roles and I took care of the musical portion of the evening. Close to eighty percent of the musical participants were clients of CNIB. Three hundred and seven ticketholders became the audience for our mock "live radio show."

Organizing events such as this gave me a sense of worth and let me feel like I was part of the universe once again. I enjoyed working with my brother Jack because he was reliable and easy to be around. He really was a man of his word. We loved to sit around and bounce ideas off each other in the planning stages. Some of the ideas we came up with were quite wild, which shows we're from the same family tree.

Jack and I were both familiar with special event planning and I wanted to try to organize the event with no vision, just to see if I could, to see how the process would be different based on this new disability. But I don't think I would have taken on this huge event without Jack at my side.

Jack was great to work with. Whenever I asked him to do something, he would say, "Yes, no problem. I've got it covered." And he really meant it. I hope that when he says, "Hey Chris, can you take care of this?" and I say, "No problem, Jack," he feels just as assured as I do.

When I was approached by the musicians, they asked what we would like them to perform. I told them to play anything as long as it was Canadian. It didn't matter

With my brother Jack, hosting the Golden Days of Canadian Radio in 2007

whether it was original or just covered by a Canadian artist. The variety that came out included everything from a French folk band and aboriginal dancers, to Gordon Lightfoot and Anne Murray covers. We really held true to the word "variety" in our variety show. Even our sponsors came out, and they loved it. They had a great time and even asked when we would do it again! They, too, were all Canadian, and their companies got to be part of the show through the cheesy commercials.

Another reason for the success of the evening was the silent auction, for which we had ten prizes. I tried to stay within the Canadian theme we had chosen. The first basket contained items from every province in Canada. I know it sounds goofy, but people went crazy over it. They thought it was goofy, too.

I never want to forget my volunteers that night. They were awesome. They made the night run smoothly. A lot of the volunteers were my family and friends.

We were able to raise just over five thousand dollars, which translated into audiobook readers, which were given to CNIB clients who could not otherwise afford them. Their cost was just shy of five hundred dollars each.

This was truly a great Jack and Chris endeavour.

16.

LOST?

"Sad Songs Say So Much" (Sir Elton John)

I'm going to talk about... how shall I say it? I'm not going to pussy foot around, I'm going to say it... I'm going to talk about death. There, I've said it. I know a lot of people who read this, including my friends and family, might be surprised—even upset—that I'm talking about it, but I'm not going to lie. I'm going to keep it real. Death has crossed my mind more than once during this entire ordeal through the years. In respect to my own mortality, I can't help but think how easy life would be for my husband and family without me around. If I wasn't here, bills wouldn't be an issue for Barry, as they do pile up. When they come up, it's always at the back of my mind. I see myself as being high maintenance at times, a burden to him, to my family, and to society. Holy drama, I know, but these feelings are very real, very strong, and at times I slap myself in the head for having them.

These feelings are strongest when I can't do something as simple as, oh, I don't know, getting ready for an event with a friend. Let's say you're going to a movie and you've planned it for a week. Your friend goes to work, and maybe has children and a life. I get that, I really do, but I don't have a life other than what you've read, so I'm looking forward to this one particular day. So, when the day comes and I get the call that one of their kids is sick and they can't make it or they have to work overtime or they're just way too tired and just really exhausted and they want to do this another night, I get that. I really do, and I really, really try not to let the disappointment come through in my voice (although I'm probably not very good at it anymore; it just gets harder and harder to mask).

I am sad, and it's almost despair, because you can't help but take it personally.

Even though it might be a particular friend this week, it was done by a different friend or family member the week before. It's not a conspiracy, and I know that in the back of my head, but it all piles up. After a while, you start believing that it is a conspiracy, in the wee hours of the morning.

17.

Diagnosis—Neuromyelitis Optica (NMO)

"Hit Me With Your Best Shot" (Pat Benatar)

May of 2008 was the start of what was to become an interesting year...

May

5th   I woke up with my entire upper torso feeling a sensation similar to a sunburn.

7th   I had a massage which concentrated on my back. The doctors thought my lymph nodes were inflamed. This didn't do anything to relieve the burning sensation.

8th   I saw Dr. N, who took some blood and started me on amitriptyline.

11th   The sunburn feeling subsided, for the most part.
14th   I woke up to discover that my legs felt like I had goose bumps all over them which were painful to touch. This feeling lasted nearly twelve hours.
15th   Dr. N informed me that my blood work was good. I told her about the feeling in my legs the day prior, and she thought I should see Dr. M.
16th   When I woke up, my right toe and the ball of my foot were numb. This had happened a few times before and eventually went away. Throughout the day, the numbness started working up my leg. Around 4:00 p.m., I was at physiotherapy at the hospital and they saw that my leg was swollen around my ankle. They did a hot/cold test. I could feel the touch, but not the cold or hot. The right side of my foot and leg was very painful to any touch.

After trying to get a hold of Dr. M and Dr. N with no success, the physiotherapists decided to take me to

Emergency to be checked out. There, a nurse took blood and a doctor consulted with the on-call neurologist. They had no idea what was happening but were quick to blame the symptoms on lupus. They couldn't proceed until the blood work results came back, and told me it may take a few days. I therefore went home. The doctor gave me a prescription for a drug called Lyrica (Pregabalin), to help with the pain in my leg.

17th — The sensation continued to affect my foot and leg and moved up to include the thigh and buttock. This was still only on my right side. I took a shower and the water on my leg was painful.

18th — The sensation in my leg continued, but was not as pronounced. Walking on the linoleum kitchen floor, I could not feel the coldness on my foot. It wasn't so much painful as irritating, like my foot felt asleep.

25th-ish — Dr. M conducted a couple of reflex and nerve conduction tests. The tests were negative, so he scheduled an MRI for August.

August

5th   I saw Dr. N to ask for help with pain and sleep management. The burning sensation had returned and was affecting my left arm from my clavicle to my wrist. In addition to the burning feeling, the muscles in that area were very painful. Dr. N prescribed Amitriptyline, Tylenol 3, and Lyrica.

9th   I continued to experience pain as I waited for an MRI on August 19.

11th   The painful area now included the front of my chest, pectoral region and breast, the back near the shoulder blade, the left side of my head and neck, and down my left shoulder to my hand. The numbness was confined to on parts of my arm and shoulder. I could feel touch, but no cold or hot sensations. All of this pain was affected just the left side of my body.

Diagnosis—Neuromyelitis Optica (NMO)

12th I was still having trouble sleeping, as the pain woke me up at night. On this particular morning, I had incredible pain in my left pectoral and forearm. The pain in the forearm was muscular, while the pectoral pain was like sunburn.

13th I really needed a distraction from recent events, so I went out for lunch with my friend Wanda. While we were eating, I noticed my left leg and left arm growing increasingly numb, which made holding a fork difficult. I called Dr. N's office, and the receptionist with whom I have a good rapport was able to book me an appointment at 3:00 p.m. that same day. She knew I wouldn't have called unless it was serious. My friend Wanda was kind enough to take me to the appointment as soon as we finished eating.

By the time I got to see Dr. N, the pain included both arms and my entire back. My right foot had gone numb.

The right pectoral and left breast were still burning, which also included the left shoulder blade. She wrote me a letter and sent me to Emergency. Once I got to see a doctor, he was also concerned. He gave me Percocet to help with the pain and then called Dr. M to consult. Dr. M ordered steroids, which I took intravenously while in hospital, and orally to take home for a week. He also wanted to see me in his office the next day. He said the problem may be related to my spine.

14th   I had an appointment with Dr. M and he wanted to wait to see the results from my MRI, still scheduled for August 19. For the time being, I was to continue the current drug regimen.

19th   I had the MRI.

29th   I saw Dr. M regarding the MRI results. The MRI report mentioned inflammation along my spine. Dr. M told me that this was most likely related to lupus vasculitis. He referred me to see Dr. G.

September

5th   I saw Dr. G, who was not satisfied with the diagnosis of lupus vasculitis, which the MRI report had stated was only one of several possibilities. He wanted more possibilities eliminated before treating me for lupus vasculitis, which would involve heavy chemotherapy. He called Dr. N to talk about options, including a lumbar puncture.

10th   I saw Dr. N, and she put in a request for a lumbar puncture to be performed at the hospital.

11th   The receptionist from Dr. N's office called with my lumbar puncture appointment, scheduled for Tuesday, September 16. Dr. N would try to arrange additional tests to be performed while I was at the hospital.

16th   This was the beginning of a three-week stay at the hospital. By this time, the pain had eased up considerably in the areas from the waist down.

However, I was still experiencing extreme pain in the left side of my back, shoulder, and my entire left arm. I was experiencing shock-like sensations, starting at my wrist and moving up to my elbow. When I leaned my head forward, a sensation travelled down my spine, then along my left leg; this instantly put my foot to sleep. I had the lumbar puncture and tests came back negative for any infection.

I saw Dr. P, who sent a blood sample of mine to the Mayo clinic to test for the NMO antibody. He was leaning towards a diagnosis of neuromyelitis optica, and this blood test could confirm his theory.[9] Over the

---

9 "Neuromyelitis optica, also known as Devic disease (DD), is a chronic disorder of nerve tissue characterized by inflammation of the optic nerve (optic neuritis) and inflammation of the spinal cord (myelitis). There appear to be two forms of this disease. In the classical, but less common type, there is a series of attacks over a short period of time (days or weeks) but, after the initial outburst, there are seldom repeat incidents. The second form is more common and is

Diagnosis—Neuromyelitis Optica (NMO)

next three weeks, while waiting for the test results, I went through three days of intravenous steroids. Lyrica was swapped out for Gabapentin (Lyrica didn't seem to be helping), and then I had five plasmapheresis treatments.

During this period, I had consults with Drs. M, P, B, F, and N. Finally, the hospital's head of neurology walked into my room. He introduced himself for the first time and said that he had some unfortunate news: I had tested positive for neuromyelitis optica (NMO). This neurological condition causes lesions to form along the spine and optic nerve. These lesions press up against nerve endings, which

---

characterized by repeated attacks separated by periods of remission. In this form, the interval between attacks may be weeks, months or years. In its early stages, Devic disease may be confused with multiple sclerosis" (from "Neuromyelitis Optica," WebMD, September 17, 2013 [http://www.webmd.com/brain/devic-disease]).

result in paralysis in certain limbs. In my specific case, NMO had contributed to my blindness; it wasn't optic neuritis, as was previously thought. To be honest, I really didn't care which diagnosis had taken my sight. It was what it was. My concern was how this new diagnosis would affect me for the rest of my life.

There are three treatments for NMO: steroids, plasmapheresis, and chemotherapy. None of these were appealing to me. This diagnosis came from the Mayo clinic, and therefore the treatments I mentioned were available at the clinic itself and here in Winnipeg. Fortunately, this meant I didn't have to physically travel to get the treatment. I started with my first of five plasmapheresis treatments.

Afterward, I was given four rounds of chemo within eight days (one every second day). The doctors were trying to control the spasms

I was experiencing in my arms and legs. When I would spasm, for example, my left arm would be pulled in tightly towards my chest. It felt like a vice grip was holding my arm against my chest. This didn't even allow me to unclench the fingers of my left hand. I would just have to wait and let it pass. These spasms/episodes/attacks could last anywhere from ten seconds to several minutes.

In addition to the above mentioned treatments, I was also prescribed a cocktail of medications. It would be months before a balance could be found in correct dosages.

October

7th The steroids and plasmapheresis had not yet made much of a difference with the pain and sensation in my left arm. The doctors next suggested that I try immunosuppressant drug therapy, which would have to be monitored closely. After talking to Dr. B, we came to a mutual agreement that the best doctors to monitor me were Dr. J and Dr. G. I scheduled appointments with both of them for November 4. I didn't want to assume this meant they agreed to monitor me through a drug trial.

27th   There had been no change since I left the hospital. The pain in my left arm was still present. The pulses or shock-like feelings still occurred along my left forearm, possibly more frequently. The sensation I was experiencing when leaning my head forward was still there. It still travelled down the spine and caused my left foot to go to sleep. My symptoms now included occasional numbness in both hands.

30th   The sunburn-like pain returned to the entire back, chest, breasts, and under both arms,

31th   My symptoms now included numbness in the left leg.

November

1st   The leg became a larger issue. From the knee to my waist, the pain was extremely bad and I felt the constant need to urinate for nearly five hours. I had one accident where I stood up and simply started to urinate and couldn't feel that I was going until it was too late. By midnight, for the most part, I had this under control.

2nd   The leg was completely numb and I was dragging it around. I wasn't very steady on my feet. The right leg was also numb, but only in a few sections of the leg. It affected areas from the middle of my calf all the way to just below my breast.

4th   I had appointment with Dr. G and Dr. J. They informed me that they would go through my files to make a list of the drugs I had been on while my eye condition was first flaring up. They would also be preparing a case to present to Manitoba Health, suggesting that I go to the Mayo Clinic in Minneapolis.

6th I called Homecare, part of the Winnipeg Regional Health Authority, to complete an intake over the phone. They told me they would call back within the next ten days to book an appointment for a home assessment.

7th The left leg was still a large issue. I was having trouble maintaining balance while on my feet. The right leg had no change.

My Extended Stay at a Rehab Hospital

For me, the rehab hospital comes with both positive and negative memories. As you can well imagine, being there 24/7 and seeing the same people for months on end, you begin to regard them as family. It's odd to think about how close we got, because in actuality we had only known each other for a few months.

There's one staff member I don't think I will ever forget. Paul was one of the physio rehab assistants. He would help to wake us up every morning. For whatever reason, this guy had a smile on his face. He would be bright-eyed and bushy-tailed. I swear he had either ten cups of coffee or ten Red Bulls before he came to our floor, because his energy level was always through the roof. I don't know if he put on that face for us, but I wondered if something was wrong with that boy. He would put a smile on our face, get us ready, and take us to our physio appointment downstairs in the gymnasium, then get us back to our rooms. He would continue bantering with us throughout the day anytime he saw us. He was the same way with everybody. He would know just when to be a smart-aleck and when to be empathetic. I guess he was in the right profession!

In life, I've learned that you have to take the good with the bad. I'll share a bad experience while in the hospital. I depended on an aide for the first while that I was in there, because I was so laid up. I was still paralyzed on one side of my body and required the use of a bedpan. I would call whenever

The Patient Patient

I had to pee, and on days that I would have chemo I was encouraged to drink more. The idea was to filter the chemo out of my body as soon as possible, which obviously meant calling for the bedpan more frequently, too. This one aide said, probably with a sigh, "Why don't you just get a catheter already!" She then put the bedpan under me and left. I started to cry.

Her remark made me feel sorry for being there. I felt I had to say something to her. It's weird when you're in the hospital by yourself. I had no family or friends there, so to say I was feeling vulnerable would be an understatement. I was blind and paralyzed and therefore needed to depend on the aides.

When she came back to get the bedpan, I asked her to come closer to the head of my bed.

"Can I tell you something?" I asked.
"Yes."
"You know what you said earlier about the catheter? I have to tell you that putting in a catheter is one of the most frightening things for me." I shed a couple of tears.

When she saw that, she apologized profusely. "Christine, I'm so sorry. I never meant that."

I hoped she might think twice next time before saying something like that to another patient. I don't know if she was busy or why she would even say that, but I felt that I needed to bring it to her attention.

The hospital had a staff member named Vi. She was the recreation coordinator for the floor I was staying on. She organized arts and crafts, movie nights, swimming, baking, etc. My favourite times with Vi were when she came to my bedside with her guitar and played songs for me. She'll never know how much it meant to me for her to take the time to make me feel better, especially with music.

I also don't want to forget to mention all the pain my physical therapist, Shelley, put me through—pain that was necessary for my recovery. I didn't swear at her once!

At some point, I realized how selfish I was being while I was in the hospital, though I didn't mean to be. For the longest time, I waited until the evening when Barry came to visit to have a shower. He would help me get a shower room and then assist me, since I didn't want anybody else helping me. The staff would ask me about taking a shower over and over again throughout the day and I would decline: "No, no. It's okay. My husband will come in the evening and he will help me." Then, when he came to visit one night, he fell asleep in the chair next to me. Out of the blue, it hit me just how selfish I was, how much I was asking of him.

The very next day, I asked the staff to put me on the shower rotation and I would just suck it up. Dignity be gone, I didn't care anymore. They staff saw a bunch of people in all shapes and sizes and they weren't going to care if they saw me naked or not; I was just going to have to get used to it so that when Barry came in the evening, we could visit as husband and wife, or even take the night off from time to time.

Another thing we had to change was our bathroom. In order for me to be able to go home, we had to make it wheelchair accessible and blind person friendly. My brothers and my brother-in-law Darrin renovated our entire bathroom, working on it in the evenings after their own fulltime jobs. I am very appreciative of their efforts.

18.

H1N1—Isolation

"All By Myself" (Eric Carmen)

One day, I came up from physio and discovered that my roommate Marge was gone. A few staff members came in to finish moving the last of her stuff. When I asked them where Marge was, they simply said she had moved to another room.

I developed a cough, which everyone took notice of and acted upon. They came to me and said, in their most endearing voices, that my ex-roommate had contracted the H1N1 virus and that they would need to test me as a precaution! They said all it would take was a swab. That didn't sound so bad, so I agreed to the test. What they failed to mention as that the swab was six inches and would go up my nose!

H1N1 seemed to have swept the globe that year, with over 214 countries reporting cases. There were over eighteen thousand deaths.

Unfortunately, the test came back positive for H1N1! I was immediately put into isolation. This meant that *anyone* coming into my room would have to wear a gown, a mask, gloves, and goggles. I was in isolation for about a month. I cannot begin to tell you how lonely that month was. I felt that if I ever experienced prison, this would be close to it.

It seemed that even the staff was coming in as little as possible. All I could imagine was a group of them outside my door playing rock-paper-scissors, with the loser having to bring in my food tray. I realized that this most likely wasn't how it happened, but that's how I felt at the time.

I can only imagine how the staff felt, or how their stomachs fell, when they saw that I had pressed the call bell when I needed the bedpan. Putting on all that gear to come into my room and help me with that had to be one of the worst parts of their job, but part of their job nonetheless.

All I can remember from physio was going through the parallel bars, hanging on. Before I got to the end, I fell and passed out. I remember waking up periodically in my bed and having a number of visitors by my bedside. I found out later that the doctors had asked Barry to ask me to get another spinal tap. They also asked Barry if I had a living will.

At Present

I'm still taking steroids and undergoing chemotherapy once every four weeks, which started when I was diagnosed in 2008. My treatment for plasmapheresis has been discontinued for the moment, due to the amount of scar tissue the doctors have run into in my neck and chest areas; they would need to put in the central line in those areas, either in my jugular vein or in my chest. The doctors and I opted to save one area in my chest for a central line, in case of emergency.

It seems that the chemo and steroids are holding the symptoms of the disease at bay. What that really means is that I'm not hospitalized! It also means that I'm ninety pounds overweight from the steroids. I'm not going to blame it all on the steroids. I'm home alone a lot, so the boredom pushes me to eat. When you don't feel good about yourself and you have no hair because of the chemo, food is a very good ally. I try not to use it as an excuse. I'm not going to lose any great amount of weight overnight, but at least I'm aware of it. So we will continue with these lines of treatments, because my body seems to be tolerating the chemo and steroids. There are no other treatments out there.

It doesn't sound fair, and we go by the seat of our pants. This is what the disease is all about. ***It is extremely rare.*** The doctors can only go by what they know. I can't expect more. I have been blessed with very good doctors. I'll never complain about the care that I have received thus far and hope to continue to have.

There is another name for this disease: it's called Devic's Disease, named after the doctor who studied cases in 1894. I was feeling like a freak when the doctor told me that I had this condition that I'd never heard of. I tried to go on the Internet to find some information. I found some, but when I tried to find local support groups, there weren't any.

I'm all for being special, and I can joke about being unique and rare, but at the end of the day, it's nice to have company. It's nice to have support and have someone who can relate to me in some way, shape, or form.

Unfortunately, a friend of mine, Monique, was diagnosed with NMO a few months ago and I couldn't tell you the odds of her being diagnosed with that—we should have bought a lottery ticket that week, because we would have won. Maybe we were destined to meet, because we needed each other. I don't know. Whatever the reason, I'm glad that I know her. And I'm hoping that she's glad she knows me, because I don't know what this disease has in store for me in the future, and I don't know what it holds for her, either. I worry about her. We can worry together, be strong about it, and hope.

Epilogue

"I Can See Clearly Now" (The Holly Cole Trio)

I admit that I'm overwhelmed with emotions and fear, and I will be for quite some time. With each loss, be it a death in the family, my vision, or my independence, I try to be smart about it. I keep telling myself that these feelings are perfectly normal to have in my situation and that time will heal all.

When people find out about my experiences, a majority say they can't imagine themselves remaining sane through it all. I disagree with them, because we all have built-in coping mechanisms. We do find a way to deal. I found music was and continues to be a great source of stress relief for me. Sometimes, after Barry leaves for work, I put on the raunchiest music I can find and

Barry and me with Gozer and Merlin, 1993

just crank it. Maybe some Pat Benatar, Joan Jett, or even Queen. Then I start howling the tune as best I can remember it. I really believe doing this has helped me release some of the stress I was harbouring.

Despite all the havoc in my life, I have tried to maintain a positive attitude along the way. Don't get me wrong, I have had my share of pity parties. Then I ask myself, "Where will self-pity get me?" There is always someone out there worse off than me and with less support than I have. Learn to recognize and concentrate on your blessings rather than focusing on your struggles in life.

I have, in essence, come to terms with the fact that there are no known cures for my illnesses. I am not in control of many things, but I *am* in control of the attitude I choose to face my obstacles with.

"I am in the pilot seat of a plane. I'll never be able to predict the weather, but I will face every day as a good day for flying."

—Christine Bonnett

Acknowledgements

I want to say, to this group of people... A special thank you, for without your support, this book would not have come to be.

Bob Campbell
Claudette DuPont
Danna Slessor-Cobb
Debbi Chodyniecki
Debbie Sontag
Gayle McPherson
Jack and Sabrina Slessor
Jennifer Cobb
Kevin Stewart
Linda Fitzpatrick
Liz Moore
Matthew Di Ubaldo
Mom and Woody Bonnett
Sandy Walker
Sharon Park
Sharon Slessor
Susan Elsey
Tamara Schaab-Johnson
Wanda Jones
The CNIB Friday coffee group
and the Winnipeg East AM Rotary Club